Photo·Guide to the OLD TESTAMENT

LION PUBLISHING

Lion Publishing
29-33 Lower Kings Rd
Berkhamsted, Herts, UK

Photographs and notes by
David Alexander

First edition 1973

International Standard Book Number 0 85648 008 8

Printed in Great Britain by
Purnell and Sons Ltd, Paulton

Introduction

It is a rewarding experience to be able to visit the Middle East, and see for oneself the places where the events of the Bible took place. But many of the Old Testament sites are not on the main tourist routes – and in any case not many will have the good fortune to be able to make such a trip at all.

This book will help fill the need. The pictures recapture the way of life and events so graphically described in the Old Testament. They open a window on the history, literature and environment of Bible times. They show the relevance of some of the archaeological discoveries made over the last century which bring us face to face with the ancient civilizations flourishing in Bible times.

The Old Testament spans the ages, from the beginning of time to the dark days after the fall of Jerusalem, the exile of God's people to Babylon and their return. The narrative ranges from history to poetry, from law to prophecy. Written over more than a thousand years, it both reflects the age in which it was written and carries a power which makes it relevant to all time.

The fact that the Old Testament so often reflects contemporary life means that our understanding of it can be helped as we see it against its background. The life of the desert tent-dwellers enables us to picture Abraham and the patriarchs. The cracked, sun-bleached salt rocks near the Dead Sea evoke the catastrophe which overwhelmed Sodom and Gomorrah. The mountains of Sinai and barren wastes of the Negev desert vividly reflect the setting of the wanderings in the wilderness and giving of the law.

Some of the sites have an interest which is more directly historical. Today there may be no more than a litter of ruins and fallen stones: but these are the actual remains of Shiloh or Shechem, Lachish or Gezer. Some of the archaeological sites are easier to imagine as they appeared in Bible times: Jericho, or Megiddo, with its Canaanite 'high place' and buildings from the time of Solomon, or Hazor with its gateway and pillars — and even a wall hastily built because of impending invasion. The Old Testament is not a collection of myths. It was about real people living in real places whose remains can still be seen today. The narrative has, in fact, at many places been shown to be reliable and relevant by modern discoveries. The historical accuracy of the Bible has been rediscovered too by many who read it in the light of contemporary research.

A shepherd leading his flock, gazelles on the mountains, wool being dyed scarlet, water in the desert, the cedars of Lebanon . . . much of the familiar language of the Old Testament lives afresh when it is pictured in this way. Today it is only in traditional areas that one can still see the wooden plough, the camel market, the flocks round a well, so it is good that as city life and mechanization increase the traditional setting of biblical life can be recorded and appreciated while it is still possible.

The main aim of this book is to encourage the reader to turn again to the whole Bible for himself. There he will see God in action with real people in actual situations. God who called out a people to live in faith in himself, who delivered them from slavery and showed them the way to live, is the same God as the God and Father of Jesus Christ, who showed the way to newness of life and won man's freedom by his death and resurrection. It is this faith, the theme of this book, which is so vital and relevant today.

Donald J. Wiseman
Professor of Assyriology in the
University of London

Contents

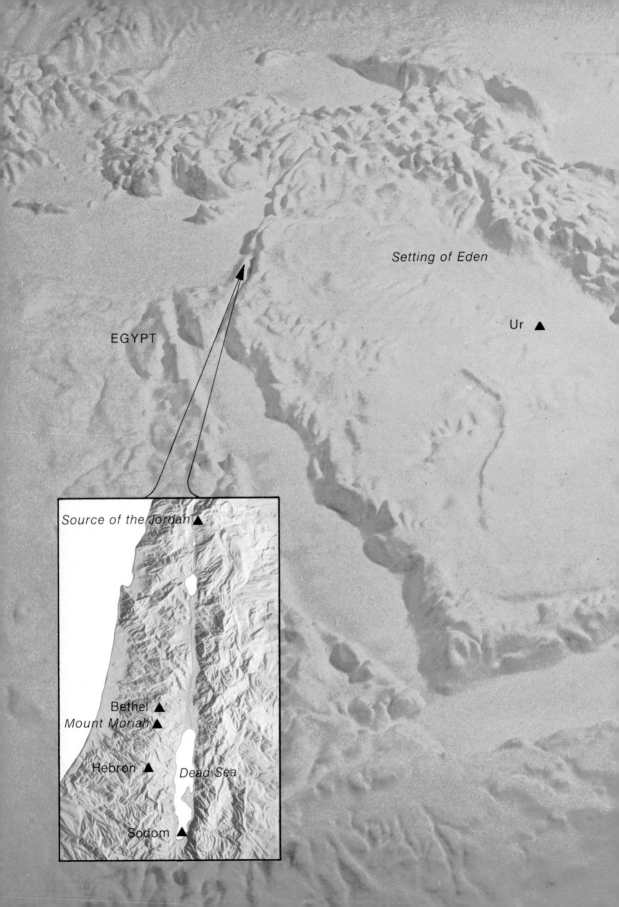

Setting of Eden

Ur ▲

EGYPT

Source of the Jordan ▲

Bethel ▲
Mount Moriah ▲

Hebron ▲   Dead Sea

Sodom ▲

PART ONE

Fathers of a Nation

Creation

*'In the beginning God created the
heavens and the earth . . .'* Genesis 1: 1

Ancient Israel extended 'from Dan to
Beersheba'. Near Dan in the extreme
north is the source of the River Jordan.
The water is forced through the stones
with an energy and power that makes it
immediately a rushing stream. Genesis 1
proclaims God as source and maker of
all things. The teeming universe sprang
from his command with all the energy
and life of a mountain stream. Presented
as a drama in six acts, God's creativity
culminated in the creation of man. And
on the seventh day he rested.

Eden

*'Then the Lord God formed man of dust
from the ground, and breathed into his
nostrils the breath of life; and man
became a living being. And the Lord
God planted a garden in Eden, in the
east; and there he put the man whom
he had formed. And out of the ground
the Lord God made to grow every tree
that is pleasant to the sight and good
for food, the tree of life also in the midst
of the garden, and the tree of the
knowledge of good and evil.'* Genesis 2: 7-9

The picture was taken further down
the Jordan River, south of the Lake
of Galilee. Eden itself was given a setting
'in the east', the rivers watering it
evoking the richness of the Mesopotamian
basin before man made it a desert. For
man chose independence of God rather
than dependence on him. He disobeyed
him to win freedom, but lost the freedom
of being the man he was made to be.
Inevitably, fellowship with God was
broken; cut off from God, the source of
life, man and all creation was turned from
good to evil.

The call of Abraham

'Now the Lord said to Abram, "Go from your country and your kindred and your father's house to the land that I will show you. And I will make of you a great nation, and I will bless you, and make your name great, so that you will be a blessing . . ." So Abram went, as the Lord had told him . . . And Abram took Sarai his wife, and Lot his brother's son, and all their possessions . . . and they set forth to go to the land of Canaan.'
Genesis 12: 1-5

God's way of making a new start was by calling one man. From him was to come a great people. Abraham left a brilliant civilization, Ur of the Chaldees, for a nomad life, in obedience to God's call. The bedouin sheikh pictured here shows how the desert 'dwellers in tents' have lived for centuries. Using goats' skins in winter and sack-cloth in the heat of summer, their tents are spread with carpets. The men recline on cushions round the earth fire-place. A more settled way of life would not enable them to find the best grazing for their livestock, their means of livelihood. So closely interdependent were animals and men in the nomad encampment that it was said of Abraham, 'he had sheep, oxen, he-asses, menservants, maid-servants, she-asses, and camels.'

Abraham and Lot

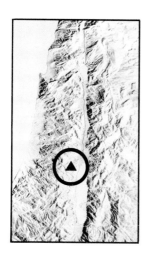

'Then Abram said to Lot, "Let there be no
strife between you and me, and between
your herdsmen and my herdsmen; for we
are kinsmen. Is not the whole land before
you? Separate yourself from me. If you
take the left hand, then I will go to the
right; or if you take the right hand, then
I will go to the left." And Lot lifted up
his eyes, and saw that the Jordan valley
was well watered everywhere like the
garden of the Lord . . . So Lot chose for
himself all the Jordan valley, and Lot
journeyed east; thus they separated from
each other. Abram dwelt in the land of
Canaan, while Lot dwelt among the cities
of the valley and moved his tent as far
as Sodom. Now the men of Sodom were
wicked, great sinners against the Lord.'
Genesis 13: 8-13*

Famine had driven Abraham and his
family to Egypt. On his return to Canaan
after the long, weary trek up through the
Negev desert, he was rich in flocks and
herds and tents, but the herdsmen were
quarrelling bitterly. The only way was to
separate. Abraham would rather have the
hard life and poor grazing on the
mountains of Judea than the richness of
the valley if it was only to cause bitterness
and family feud. It also says something
for Abraham's attitude that he allowed
his younger nephew first choice. Lot's
decision, as it turned out, was a moral
one. The rich cities of the plain had the
tempting night-life. Lot journeyed east.

Hebron

'The Lord said to Abram, after Lot had separated from him, "Lift up your eyes, and look from the place where you are, northward and southward and eastward and westward; for all the land which you see I will give to you and to your descendants for ever. I will make your descendants as the dust of the earth; so that if one can count the dust of the earth, your descendants also can be counted. Arise, walk through the length and the breadth of the land, for I will give it to you." So Abram moved his tent, and came and dwelt by the oaks of Mamre, which are at Hebron; and there he built an altar to the Lord.'
Genesis 13: 14-18

Hebron stands at a height of over 3,000 feet in the mountains south of Jerusalem. The Arabic name for Abraham is al-Khalil er-Rahman, the Friend of the Lord, hence the Arabic name for Hebron—Khalil. Abraham bought a plot of ground with a cave here, as a family burying-ground. He bought it from Hittites who were settled in the area, and the details of the negotiations recorded in Genesis 23 reflect the intricacies of Hittite laws and customs of the time. The burial-place. the Cave of Machpelah, is now a shrine. The building over it, pictured here, goes back to the time of Herod, with additions in Byzantine and Crusader times. Mamre, where Abraham lived, is a mile or two south of Hebron.

Mount Moriah

'After these things God tested Abraham, and said to him, "Abraham!" And he said, "Here am I." He said, "Take your son, your only son Isaac, whom you love, and go to the land of Moriah, and offer him there as a burnt offering upon one of the mountains of which I shall tell you." So Abraham rose early in the morning, saddled his ass, and took two of his young men with him, and his son Isaac; and he cut the wood for the burnt offering, and arose and went to the place of which God had told him. On the third day Abraham lifted up his eyes and saw the place afar off. Then Abraham said to his young men, "Stay here with the ass; I and the lad will go yonder and worship, and come again to you."'
Genesis 22: 1-5

At Mamre God had told Sarah she would have a child—and she had laughed in sheer disbelief, for she was past the age for child-bearing. Yet God had promised that Abraham's descendants would be like the stars in number, and like the sand on the sea-shore. The child Isaac was God's fulfilment of his own promise. So when God then seemed to be calling Abraham to the mountains of Moriah to sacrifice his son, the realization of God's own promise, it was a supreme test of Abraham's trust in God's promises as well as his natural love for his son. Abraham's faith was vindicated: a ram caught in a thicket was provided for the sacrifice instead of Isaac. The mountains of Moriah were also to be the site of Solomon's Temple (2 Chronicles 3: 1): the rocky top of the temple hill is enshrined in the Mosque of Omar which stands there now.

The Dead Sea

'Then the men said to Lot, "Have you anyone else here? Sons-in-law, sons, daughters, or any one you have in the city, bring them out of the place; for we are about to destroy this place, because the outcry against its people has become great before the Lord, and the Lord has sent us to destroy it."
Genesis 19: 12, 13

The site of the cities of Sodom and Gomorrah is thought to be now covered by the waters of the south end of the Dead Sea. Certainly the acrid reek in the air and the rocks bare of vegetation evoke the catastrophe which overwhelmed the cities whose corruption made them fit only for destruction. The Dead Sea, or Salt Sea, lies at the deepest point in the long rift valley down which flows the River Jordan. As the heat of the sun evaporates the water, the concentrates of potash and other chemicals build up to amount to 25 per cent of the water content.

Pillars of salt

'Then the Lord rained on Sodom and Gomorrah brimstone and fire from the Lord out of heaven; and he overthrew those cities, and all the valley, and all the inhabitants of the cities, and what grew on the ground. But Lot's wife behind him looked back, and she became a pillar of salt.'
Genesis 19: 24-26

Lot escaped alive only because of Abraham's pleading before God. His wife, hankering for the old life, was overwhelmed like the victims of Vesuvius at Pompeii. The great pillars of salt at the south end of the lake bear silent witness both to God's judgement in destruction and to his mercy in answering Abraham's prayer.

A wife for Isaac

'Then the servant took ten of his master's camels and departed, taking all sorts of choice gifts from his master; and he arose, and went to Mesopotamia, to the city of Nahor. And he made the camels kneel down outside the city by the well of water at the time of evening, the time when women go out to draw water. And he said, "O Lord, God of my master Abraham, grant me success today, I pray thee, and show steadfast love to my master Abraham. Behold, I am standing by the spring of water, and the daughters of the men of the city are coming out to draw water. Let the maiden to whom I shall say, 'Pray let down your jar that I may drink,' and who shall say, 'Drink, and I will water your camels' — let her be the one whom thou hast appointed for thy servant Isaac. By this I shall know that thou hast shown steadfast love to my master." Before he had done speaking, behold, Rebekah . . . came out with her water jar upon her shoulder.' Genesis 24: 10-15

Abraham sent his chief steward to his own home-country to seek a wife for his son Isaac. The steward's prayer was answered: Rebekah was the daughter of Abraham's nephew, and, as it turned out, a wife whom Isaac truly loved.

Bethel

'Jacob left Beer-sheba, and went toward Haran. And he came to a certain place, and stayed there that night, because the sun had set. Taking one of the stones of the place, he put it under his head and lay down in that place to sleep. And he dreamed that there was a ladder set up on the earth, and the top of it reached to heaven; and behold, the angels of God were ascending and descending on it! And behold, the Lord stood above it and said, "I am the Lord, the God of Abraham your father and the God of Isaac; the land on which you lie I will give to your descendants; your descendants shall be like the dust of the earth . . ." So Jacob rose early in the morning, and he took the stone which he had put under his head and set it up for a pillar and poured oil on the top of it. He called the name of the place Bethel.' Genesis 28: 10-19

'Bethel' means 'House of God'. At first sight it hardly seemed that to a lonely, miserable young man leaving home. It was an area of steep, stony, forbidding hills and valleys. But in his dream the stony hill became a staircase filled with the messengers of God. In the morning the rock which was his pillow was set up as an altar to God. For there God renewed the promise made to Jacob's father. Bethel was later to play a major role in Israel's history: the resting-place of the ark, a sanctuary visited by Samuel and later adopted by Jeroboam as a sanctuary for the northern kingdom to rival Jerusalem.

Grain in Egypt

'When Jacob learned that there was grain in Egypt, he said to his sons, "Why do you look at one another?" And he said, "Behold, I have heard that there is grain in Egypt; go down and buy grain for us there, that we may live, and not die." So ten of Joseph's brothers went down to buy grain in Egypt. But Jacob did not send Benjamin, Joseph's brother, with his brothers, for he feared that harm might befall him. Thus the sons of Israel came to buy among the others who came, for the famine was in the land of Canaan. Now Joseph was governor over the land; he it was who sold to all the people of the land . . .'
Genesis 42: 1-6

A rural economy was a precarious one: lack of rain and a poor harvest soon caused hardship and famine. Refugees from famine would pour into the areas known to be better off. Joseph, the insufferable younger brother sold into slavery years before, now had power of life and death over the brothers who had wronged him. For Joseph had had the forethought and administrative skill to store grain from the good years in preparation for the bad. From being a slave he became second only to Pharaoh. But the good fortune of the children of Israel in Egypt was not to last. After Joseph's death they were increasingly enslaved, burdened under their task-masters, crying out for deliverance.

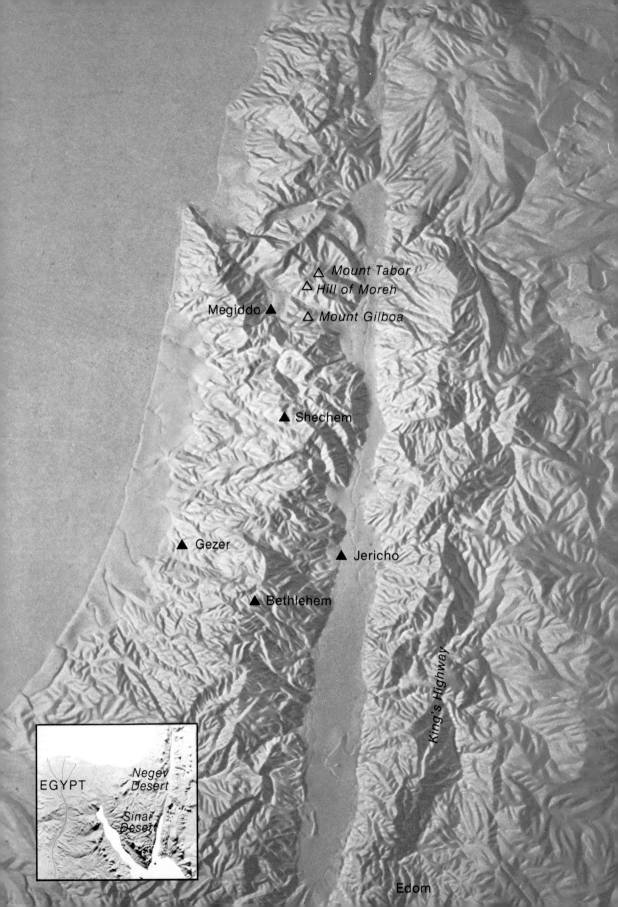

△ *Mount Tabor*
△ *Hill of Moreh*

Megiddo ▲

△ *Mount Gilboa*

▲ Shechem

▲ Gezer

▲ Jericho

▲ Bethlehem

King's Highway

EGYPT

*Negev
Desert*

*Sinai
Desert*

Edom

PART TWO

Freedom and a New Life

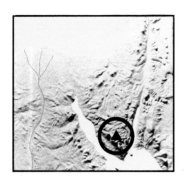

The call of Moses

'Now Moses was keeping the flock of his father-in-law, Jethro, the priest of Midian; and he led his flock to the west side of the wilderness, and came to Horeb, the mountain of God. And the angel of the Lord appeared to him in a flame of fire out of the midst of a bush; and he looked, and lo, the bush was burning, yet it was not consumed. And Moses said, "I will turn aside and see this great sight, why the bush is not burnt." When the Lord saw that he turned aside to see, God called to him out of the bush, "Moses, Moses!" And he said, "Here am I." . . .'
Exodus 3: 1-4

Moses was far from the court of Pharaoh, the place of his upbringing. Taking the law into his own hands, he had struck a blow for his people's freedom — but the only result was his own retreat to the desert of Sinai. It was there, many years later, that God revealed himself to Moses: the God of his fathers, the God whose name was 'I AM WHO I AM', the God who would not only deliver his people but would call and equip Moses to be the instrument of deliverance.

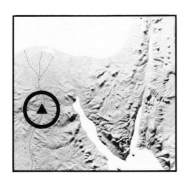

A plague of locusts

'Moses stretched forth his rod over the land of Egypt, and the Lord brought an east wind upon the land all that day and all that night; and when it was morning the east wind had brought the locusts. And the locusts came up over all the land of Egypt, and settled on the whole country of Egypt, such a dense swarm of locusts as had never been before, nor ever shall be again. For they covered the face of the whole land, so that the land was darkened, and they ate all the plants in the land and all the fruit of the trees . . .' Exodus 10: 13-15

Pharaoh would not let the people of Israel go. One plague followed another. Pharaoh realized only too well that he was fighting God himself. But he only hardened his heart still further. And the great natural catastrophes went on, one inexorably leading onto the next: an abnormally high Nile, bringing down red earth and deadly bacteria, would kill the fish. Frogs left the polluted river to plague the land, and from their rotting carcases came plagues of mosquitoes, flies and the cattle pest on the cattle in the fields. So it went on: the locusts were blown in on the wind to devastate the land afresh. Pharaoh — a god to his people because of his apparent control over the regular seasons of the Nile — was no match for the Lord of heaven and earth.

The wilderness

*'And the people murmured against Moses
and said, "Why did you bring us up out
of Egypt, to kill us and our children
and our cattle with thirst?" So Moses cried
to the Lord . . .'* Exodus 17: 3, 4

The Sinai peninsula is mountainous,
rocky desert. Temperatures soar under
the hot sun. The glorious deliverance from
Egypt was soon forgotten as the people
faced the harsh realities of lack of water
and food. But God showed that he would
sustain those he saved: he showed
Moses the water-bearing rock at Horeb.
He sent quails, flocks of migrating birds
easy to catch for food. He sent manna, a
small, white, honey-tasting substance.
Tempted in the wilderness, Jesus took
on his lips the key phrases of the
experience of Israel: including the fact
that man does not live by bread alone,
but by every word that comes from the
mouth of God.

Sinai

*'On the morning of the third day there
were thunders and lightnings, and a
thick cloud upon the mountain, and a
very loud trumpet blast, so that all the
people who were in the camp trembled.
Then Moses brought the people out of
the camp to meet God; and they took
their stand at the foot of the mountain.*
Exodus 19: 16, 17

God did not leave his people to wander
without guidance and direction. His
presence went with them by night and
day. He also gave them, in the Ten
Commandments and in the law generally,
instructions on how to live. And in
doing so he laid down a pattern of
morality of universal significance.
The God of holiness was also a God of
love, infinitely concerned for the welfare
of his people.

Sanctuary in the wilderness

'The Lord said to Moses, ". . . Let them make me a sanctuary, that I may dwell in their midst. According to all that I show you concerning the pattern of the tabernacle, and of all its furniture, so you shall make it. They shall make an ark of acacia wood; two cubits and a half shall be its length, a cubit and a half its breadth, and a cubit and a half its height. And you shall overlay it with pure gold, within and without . . . And you shall make a table of acacia wood . . . And you shall make a lampstand of pure gold . . ." ' Exodus 25

The tabernacle, or tent, which was to be God's sanctuary in the wilderness, was modelled on other portable sanctuaries known to us from Egyptian illustrations. Many of the details symbolized the relationship of God to his people. They were also practical. The acacia tree, for instance, was one of the very few available in the desert—as is still the case today in the Negev desert and Sinai peninsula. The gold would have been beaten from the plunder taken out of Egypt; silver, jewellery, linen and other materials also brought from Egypt; the main goat-hair covering made from the skins of their flocks.

A pagan altar

'And the Lord said to Moses, "Say to the people of Israel, I am the Lord your God. You shall not do as they do in the land of Egypt, where you dwelt, and you shall not do as they do in the land of Canaan, to which I am bringing you . . ." "Say to the people of Israel, Any man of the people of Israel, or of the strangers that sojourn in Israel, who gives any of his children to Molech shall be put to death; the people of the land shall stone him with stones. I myself will set my face against that man, and will cut him off from among his people, because he has given one of his children to Molech, defiling my sanctuary and profaning my holy name." ' Leviticus 18: 1-3; 20: 1-3

The law was given not only for Israel's present but also for the future. And it prepared the people not only for a new life in the promised land but for a fight for survival. The picture here is of an altar to the god Moloch, or Molech, at Byblos, Lebanon. The stone enclosure was for child-sacrifice. Nearby stand receptacles for the blood and for the rest of the disgusting pagan ritual. God's concern to keep his people from moral pollution was no mere sentiment. Physical death was preferable to the corruption of his people and the end of his whole plan of salvation for them and for the world. The destruction of the Canaanites was not out of concern for racial purity but a matter of judgement on utter corruption. The Amorites had been given 400 years to mend their ways (Genesis 15: 16).

A law of love

'You shall not steal, nor deal falsely, nor lie to one another. And you shall not swear by my name falsely, and so profane the name of your God: I am the Lord. You shall not oppress your neighbour or rob him. The wages of a hired servant shall not remain with you all night until the morning. You shall not curse the deaf or put a stumbling block before the blind, but you shall fear your God: I am the Lord. You shall do no injustice in judgment; you shall not be partial to the poor or defer to the great, but in righteousness shall you judge your neighbour. You shall not go up and down as a slanderer among your people, and you shall not stand forth against the life of your neighbour: I am the Lord.'
Leviticus 19: 11-16

The law was moral, ceremonial and social. Detailed laws of food and hygiene reflect the climate and other local conditions in their concern for the people's health. Laws were designed to promote social justice, to safeguard the weak against exploitation by the rich, to protect those who could not protect themselves. Laws for the use of the land were designed for its conservation and highest productivity. The local applications may not be relevant in other countries and at other times, but the basic concern must be the same: loving the Lord our God must result in loving our neighbour as ourselves.

A law for every home

'Hear, O Israel: The Lord our God is one Lord; and you shall love the Lord your God with all your heart, and with all your soul, and with all your might. And these words which I command you this day shall be upon your heart . . . And you shall write them on the doorposts of your house and on your gates.'
Deuteronomy 6: 4-9

In literal obedience to the command, Jewish households have traditionally put this passage and the similar one in Deuteronomy 11: 13-21 in a box attached to the door-post. Called a 'Mezuzah', it seems that it was introduced by the Hasidim Jews in the second century BC in order to counter the increasing influence of Hellenistic Greek culture.

The King's Highway

'Moses sent messengers from Kadesh to the king of Edom, . . . "Now let us pass through your land. We will not pass through field or vineyard, neither will we drink water from a well; we will go along the King's Highway, we will not turn aside to the right hand or to the left, until we have passed through your territory."'
Numbers 20: 14-17

The picture shows the view the messengers would have had, looking across to the mountains of Edom. Moses' plan was to strike across to the main north-south highway which ran through Edomite territory: but Edom would not have it. The frustration and constant delay and further wandering in the desert must have seemed interminable.

Jericho

'On the seventh day they rose early at the dawn of day, and marched around the city in the same manner seven times . . . And at the seventh time, when the priests had blown the trumpets, Joshua said to the people, "Shout; for the Lord has given you the city . . ."'
Joshua 6: 15, 16

The forty years of wandering in the desert were over. But the entry into the promised land was not to be an easy end to all the people's problems. Jericho was only the first of the cities that had to be taken. It owed its position to its water-supply—the well that featured later in the story of Elisha. The mound of ancient Jericho, topped by the white hut, has remains going back to long before Joshua's time: it had already been destroyed and rebuilt several times, and as it was allowed to remain in ruins for centuries after Israel's attack it was unlikely to provide direct evidence of this actual incident. However, much that has been found there gives a commentary on many centuries of Old Testament history.

Gezer

'Then Horam king of Gezer came up to help Lachish; and Joshua smote him and his people, until he left none remaining. And Joshua passed on with all Israel from Lachish to Eglon; and they laid siege to it, and assaulted it; and they took it on that day, and smote it with the edge of the sword; and every person in it he utterly destroyed that day, as he had done to Lachish.' Joshua 10: 33-35

After attacking the cities near Jericho, Joshua cut across to the key fortified cities in the foothills of the mountains guarding the main highway on the plain: Lachish (see page 104) and Gezer. Among extensive ruins from this time is a complex water tunnel. Other ruins remain from the time of Solomon, who rebuilt the city. Among the objects discovered was the Gezer Calendar, a simple aid for remembering the agricultural seasons (now in the Istanbul Archaeological Museum).

Megiddo

'And these are the kings of the land whom Joshua and the people of Israel defeated on the west side of Jordan . . . the king of Jericho . . . the king of Megiddo . . . in all, thirty-one kings.'
Joshua 12: 7, 9, 21, 24

At the major archaeological site of Megiddo (see too pages 93 and 100), in one of the lowest layers uncovered, is this Canaanite altar or 'high place'. Called high places because they were originally sited on hill-tops, these pagan sanctuaries were later frequently condemned by the prophets of Israel.

Mount Tabor

'Deborah said to Barak, "Up! For this is the day in which the Lord has given Sisera into your hand. Does not the Lord go out before you?" So Barak went down from Mount Tabor with ten thousand men following him. And the Lord routed Sisera and all his chariots and all his army before Barak at the edge of the sword.' Judges 4: 14, 15

In the period of the Judges a pattern recurs: the people turn away from God; they suffer judgement in the form of invasion or enemy occupation; they cry to God for help; he raises up a deliverer to free them. The 1850-foot Mount Tabor in Galilee, with its commanding views and distinctive rounded shape, was the scene of this confrontation with the Canaanite general Sisera. Deborah's magnificent song of triumph tells what happened. It seems that a sudden cloudburst turned the Kishon brook into a raging torrent, which swept many of Sisera's chariots away. The rest, clogged in the mud, would have been an easy prey.

Gideon

'Then Gideon and all the people who were with him rose early and encamped beside the spring of Harod; and the camp of Midian was north of them, by the hill of Moreh, in the valley.' Judges 7: 1

So the drama of Gideon's attack on the hosts of the Midianites unfolds. Down in the valley below the slopes of Gilboa the pools from the waters of the spring Harod reflect the sky. There Gideon reduced his army to a small, crack fighting-force. The hill of Moreh opposite marks the place in the valley where the army of Midian was camped—and where Gideon led his surprise attack.

Shechem

*'And all the citizens of Shechem came
together, and all Beth-millo, and they
went and made Abimelech king, by the
oak of the pillar at Shechem. When it was
told to Jotham, he went and stood on the
top of Mount Gerizim, and cried aloud
and said to them, "Listen to me, you
men of Shechem, that God may listen
to you. The trees once went forth to
anoint a king over them . . ."'*
Judges 9: 6-8

At Shechem Abraham camped by 'the
oak of Moreh'. Here Jacob buried the
'strange gods', and Joseph sought his
brothers. It was the central place where
Joshua gathered the elders, just before
his death. But in the time of the Judges,
Shechem was still a centre of Canaanite
worship. A temple to Baal was destroyed
in this story, after Jotham had used his
parable to attempt to turn the people
from Abimelech. Later in Israel's history
Jeroboam I made the town his capital
for a time, and after the exile it became
the chief city of the Samaritans.
Excavations have revealed buildings
going back to Canaanite times,
including this wall and gateway.

Bethlehem

'So Naomi returned, and Ruth the Moabitess her daughter-in-law with her, who returned from the country of Moab. And they came to Bethlehem at the beginning of barley harvest . . . Then Naomi her mother-in-law said to her, "My daughter, should I not seek a home for you, that it may be well with you? Now is not Boaz our kinsman, with whose maidens you were? See, he is winnowing barley tonight at the threshing floor. Wash therefore and anoint yourself, and put on your best clothes and go down to the threshing floor . . ."'
Ruth 1: 22; 3: 1-3

Bethlehem, 'house of bread', straddles a ridge high in the hills of Judea. Naomi, with her husband and family, had had to flee from Bethlehem to Moab to escape famine. There her husband died, as did her son who married 'Ruth the Moabitess'. With a lyrical simplicity and restraint the story tells how their kinsman honoured his responsibilities towards Ruth — and only at the end do we discover that these were the ancestors of King David himself, and hence the forebears of Jesus who was born in Bethlehem, City of David. The story is set in the period of the Judges, and in its simple beauty shows something of the rural background to a time which was otherwise such a succession of upheavals and wars.

Tyre ▲

▲ Hazor

Mount Carmel △

Megiddo ▲ ▲ Jezreel

△ *Mount Gilboa*

SAMARIA

▲ Shiloh

Gezer ▲

▲ Gibeah
Kiriath-jearim ▲ ▲ **Jerusalem**

Lachish ▲

▲ Hebron

▲ Ein Gedi

PART THREE

A Nation under God

Shiloh

'Now the boy Samuel was ministering to the Lord under Eli. And the word of the Lord was rare in those days; there was no frequent vision. At that time Eli, whose eyesight had begun to grow dim, so that he could not see, was lying down in his own place; the lamp of God had not yet gone out, and Samuel was lying down within the temple of the Lord, where the ark of God was. Then the Lord called, "Samuel! Samuel!" and he said, "Here I am!" . . . And Samuel grew, and the Lord was with him and let none of his words fall to the ground. And all Israel from Dan to Beer-sheba knew that Samuel was established as a prophet of the Lord. And the Lord appeared again at Shiloh, for the Lord revealed himself to Samuel at Shiloh by the word of the Lord.' 1 Samuel 3: 1-4, 19-21

Shiloh now is no more than a ruin of stones on a hill in Samaria. At the time of the Judges it was the principal sanctuary of the Israelites. By Eli's time the tent, or tabernacle, had become some kind of temple. Here Hannah, childless and 'deeply distressed . . . prayed to the Lord, and wept bitterly', vowing to dedicate her child to the Lord if he should answer her prayer. So it was that the boy Samuel grew up in the temple, and, while there, was called to be a prophet of God at a time when 'the word of the Lord was rare'. Not long after, Shiloh was destroyed, probably by the Philistines. Jeremiah takes this as an example of God's judgement on his people's wickedness.

Kiriath-jearim

*'Then the men of Beth-shemesh said,
"Who is able to stand before the Lord,
this holy God? And to whom shall he go
up away from us?" So they sent
messengers to the inhabitants of
Kiriath-jearim, saying, "The Philistines
have returned the ark of the Lord. Come
down and take it up to you." And the
men of Kiriath-jearim came and took up
the ark of the Lord, and brought it to
the house of Abinadab on the hill; and
they consecrated his son, Eleazar, to
have charge of the ark of the Lord. From
the day that the ark was lodged at
Kiriath-jearim, a long time passed, some
twenty years, and all the house of Israel
lamented after the Lord.'*
1 Samuel 6: 20-7: 2

The ark was the symbol of God's
presence. Captured by the Philistines,
and then returned, it began its slow
journey to its final resting-place in
Jerusalem. A sharp reminder that God's
presence is utterly holy and not to be
treated casually made the men of
Beth-shemesh ask the nearby town of
Kiriath-jearim to take over the
responsibility for it. From Kiriath-jearim
the ark was eventually taken to Jerusalem
by David, with great rejoicing. The
village of Abu Gosh stands on the site
today. The hills above the village gave
pilgrims travelling from the coast their
first sight of the holy city of Jerusalem.
It became customary for Jewish pilgrims
to rend their clothes there to express
their sorrow at the destruction of
Jerusalem and its Temple.

Gibeah

'And Samuel said to all the people, "Do you see him whom the Lord has chosen? There is none like him among all the people." And all the people shouted, "Long live the king!" Then Samuel told the people the rights and duties of the kingship; and he wrote them in a book and laid it up before the Lord. Then Samuel sent all the people away, each one to his home. Saul also went to his home at Gibeah, and with him went men of valour whose hearts God had touched.'
1 Samuel 10: 24-26

Gibeah was the fortress and royal residence of Saul, as well as his home-town. It lies some three miles north of Jerusalem. On the same site King Hussein of Jordan started to build a palace, only to be overtaken by the events of the Six Day War in 1967. Excavations by W. F. Albright in 1922 brought to light a fortress, burnt near the end of the twelfth century BC, which may have been the scene of the crime described in Judges 19-20. A second level representing Saul's time included a two-storey fortress whose ground-floor storeroom contained pottery vessels of a certain simple luxury.

Ein Gedi

'When Saul returned from following the Philistines, he was told, "Behold, David is in the wilderness of Engedi." Then Saul took three thousand chosen men out of all Israel, and went to seek David and his men in front of the Wildgoats' Rocks . . . Afterward David also arose, and went out of the cave, and called after Saul, "My Lord the king!" And when Saul looked behind him, David bowed with his face to the earth, and did obeisance. And David said to Saul, "Why do you listen to the words of men who say, 'Behold, David seeks your hurt?' Lo, this day your eyes have seen how the Lord gave you today into my hand in the cave; and some bade me kill you, but I spared you. I said, 'I will not put forth my hand against my lord; for he is the Lord's anointed.' . . ."'
1 Samuel 24: 1-2, 8-10

On the west shore of the Dead Sea is a sudden burst of greenery. The fresh-water stream at Ein Gedi flows down a gorge towards the shore, making possible a patch of sub-tropical cultivation which contrasts vividly with the desert around. The area abounds in caves, ideal hide-outs for a hunted man. David, on the run from Saul, would have had no difficulty in escaping, even from 3,000 men. He would have had no difficulty, either, in finding ready imagery for his psalms. The fresh stream in the desert surroundings, the mountains, the shadow of a mighty rock, the water cascading down cataracts and waterfalls, the gazelles and wild goats, all presented vivid pictures for his poetry.

The death of Saul

'*Now the Philistines fought against Israel;
and the men of Israel fled before the
Philistines, and fell slain on Mount
Gilboa. And the Philistines overtook Saul
and his sons; and the Philistines slew
Jonathan and Abinadab and Malchishua,
the sons of Saul. The battle pressed hard
upon Saul, and the archers found him;
and he was badly wounded by the
archers. Then Saul said to his armour-
bearer, "Draw your sword, and thrust
me through with it, lest these
uncircumcised come and thrust me
through, and make sport of me." But his
armour-bearer would not; for he feared
greatly. Therefore Saul took his own
sword, and fell upon it. . . . On the
morrow, when the Philistines came to
strip the slain, they found Saul and his
three sons fallen on Mount Gilboa. And
they cut off his head, and stripped off his
armour, and sent messengers throughout
the land of the Philistines, to carry the
good news to their idols and to the
people. They put his armour in the
temple of Ashtaroth; and they fastened
his body to the wall of Beth-shan.*'
1 Samuel 31: 1-4, 8-10

The long, bitter struggle with the
Philistines led ultimately to tragedy: Saul
and Jonathan were slain on Mount Gilboa.
This view from the ancient city of
Beth-shan looks towards Gilboa in the
distance. Among the important finds were
two temples which may have been those
dedicated to Dagon and Ashtaroth in
which Saul's armour was displayed.
David's lament over Saul and Jonathan
in 2 Samuel 1 recalls their death more
personally and acutely: 'How are the
mighty fallen in the midst of battle! . . .'

Hebron

'Then all the tribes of Israel came to David at Hebron, and said, "Behold, we are your bone and flesh. In times past, when Saul was king over us, it was you that led out and brought in Israel; and the Lord said to you, 'You shall be shepherd of my people Israel, and you shall be prince over Israel.'" So all the elders of Israel came to the king at Hebron; and King David made a covenant with them at Hebron before the Lord, and they anointed David king over Israel. David was thirty years old when he began to reign, and he reigned forty years.' 2 Samuel 5: 1-15

Hebron had been the home of Abraham (see page 20). The highest town in Israel, it was now to be David's capital for seven and a half years until at last Jerusalem was taken. Later in David's reign, it was in Hebron that Absalom plotted his conspiracy against him.

Jerusalem

'And the king and his men went to Jerusalem against the Jebusites, . . . And David dwelt in the stronghold, and called it the city of David. And David built the city round about from the Millo inward. And David became greater and greater, for the Lord, the God of hosts, was with him.' 2 Samuel 5: 6-10

Looking up towards what was later to be the temple area, the view of Jerusalem from the south shows the part which was the ancient city of David. The domes above it are now those of mosques. Mount Zion may have been the whole area; today the name is given specifically to the hill on the left side of the picture (see too page 117). On the right the ground slopes away steeply to the Kidron Valley.

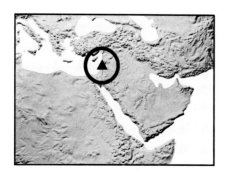

Tyre

'Now Hiram king of Tyre sent his servants to Solomon, when he heard that they had anointed him king in place of his father; for Hiram always loved David. And Solomon sent word to Hiram, "You know that David my father could not build a house for the name of the Lord his God because of the warfare with which his enemies surrounded him, until the Lord put them under the soles of his feet. But now the Lord my God has given me rest on every side; there is neither adversary nor misfortune. And so I purpose to build a house for the name of the Lord my God, as the Lord said to David my father, 'Your son, whom I will set upon your throne in your place, shall build the house for my name.' Now therefore command that cedars of Lebanon be cut for me; and my servants will join your servants, and I will pay you for your servants such wages as you set; for you know that there is no one among us who knows how to cut timber like the Sidonians."' 1 Kings 5: 1-6

Hiram, King of Tyre, had already supplied David with timber. Now at last David's son Solomon was to do what David had longed to do himself, build a 'house of the Lord'. The alliance with Tyre was a useful one. Solomon not only received cedar and cypress wood and gold. He was also given the services of a man to do all the bronze-casting for the new temple. In return, Hiram was given oil and wheat, also 'twenty cities in the land of Galilee' with which he was not particularly pleased. Tyre was at the height of its power, overshadowing its neighbour and rival, Sidon. Both towns had grown as a result of Phoenician sea-power. Originally an island, Tyre was linked to the land by a causeway at this time.

Solomon's Temple

*'In the four hundred and eightieth year
after the people of Israel came out of
the land of Egypt, in the fourth year of
Solomon's reign over Israel, in the month
of Ziv, which is the second month, he
began to build the house of the Lord.
The house which King Solomon built
for the Lord was sixty cubits long,
twenty cubits wide, and thirty cubits high.
The vestibule in front of the nave of the
house was twenty cubits long, equal to
the width of the house, and ten cubits
deep in front of the house . . .'*
1 Kings 6: 1-3

The enormous temple area dominates
the old city of Jerusalem. The rocky top
of Mount Moriah on which it was built is
now incorporated in the Mosque of Omar
(see picture, page 27). The wall pictured
here is at the highest, south-eastern end.
The recently uncovered masonry on the
right may go back to the time of
Jehoshaphat of Judah/Ahab of Israel.
Since Solomon's time, successive
generations have added, rebuilt,
destroyed and built again on the site,
until now the area incorporates building
from Crusader, Muslim, Roman and
Herodian days and further back still.

Solomon's quarries

*'When the house was built, it was with
stone prepared at the quarry; so that
neither hammer nor axe nor any tool of
iron was heard in the temple, while it was
being built.'* 1 Kings 6: 7

Why was this curious note included in the
narrative? Deep below the old city of
Jerusalem, a great cavern extends over
200 yards into the rock. The marks of the
picks used to quarry out the rock can still be
seen. Though so near to the Temple, no
sound of the underground quarrying could
carry to the actual construction site above.

Solomon's wide interests

'And God gave Solomon wisdom and understanding beyond measure, and largeness of mind like the sand on the seashore . . . He spoke of trees, from the cedar that is in Lebanon to the hyssop that grows out of the wall; he spoke also of beasts, and of birds, and of reptiles, and of fish . . . King Solomon built a fleet of ships at Ezion-geber, which is near Eloth on the shore of the Red Sea . . . Now the weight of gold that came to Solomon in one year was six hundred and thirty-six talents of gold, besides that which came from the traders and from the traffic of the merchants . . . And the whole earth sought the presence of Solomon to hear his wisdom, which God had put into his mind. Every one of them brought his present . . .'
1 Kings 4, 9, 10

Solomon was a man of many talents and wide interests. At Timna', near his port of Ezion-geber on the Red Sea, Solomon's copper-mines have been discovered. In a small valley, surrounded by the rocky hills of the Negev, the mines are being worked again today. On the top of the hill overlooking the site stood a watch-tower from which the king's men kept guard over those forced to labour in the copper-smelting pits, of which the remains can still be seen next to heaps of black slag.

The cities of Solomon

'And this is the account of the forced labour which King Solomon levied to build the house of the Lord and his own house and the Millo and the wall of Jerusalem and Hazor and Megiddo and Gezer . . . and all the store-cities that Solomon had, and the cities for his chariots, and the cities for his horsemen . . . But of the people of Israel Solomon made no slaves; they were the soldiers, they were his officials, his commanders, his captains, his chariot commanders and his horsemen.' 1 Kings 9: 15, 19, 22

With his labour-force of captives Solomon's building programme was a vigorous one. This stairway at Megiddo leads to a gateway. Those at Hazor and Gezer are built to an identical plan: striking confirmation of the accuracy of the Bible text. Built to guard the pass through the Carmel range on the main north-south coastal highway, Megiddo reflects layer after layer of Bible history (see too pages 57 and 100). Here King Josiah was killed attempting to halt Egyptian forces on their way to aid crumbling Assyria. By New Testament times, Megiddo had seen so many battles that the writer of Revelation could use its name 'Armageddon' (or 'Har-Mageddon', the Hill of Megiddo) as a symbol of war.

Contest on Carmel

'When Ahab saw Elijah, Ahab said to him, "Is it you, you troubler of Israel?" ... Ahab sent to all the people of Israel, and gathered the prophets together at Mount Carmel. And Elijah came near to all the people, and said, "How long will you go limping with two different opinions? If the Lord is God, follow him; but if Baal, then follow him."' 1 Kings 18: 17-21

A steep path leads down from the heights of Mount Carmel at its eastern end. Partway down is a natural amphitheatre. The track goes on down to the stream at the bottom. At the top of the path there is a view of the sea in one direction, the Valley of Jezreel and Galilee in the other. Rocks litter the natural theatre. Whether or not this was the exact site of Elijah's confrontation with the prophets of Baal, the conditions are right. Baal was supposed to control the elements, the rain and wind and fire. But God showed himself supreme. 'When all the people saw it, they fell on their faces; and they said, "The Lord, he is God; the Lord, he is God."'

Jezreel

'Now Naboth the Jezreelite had a vineyard in Jezreel, beside the palace of Ahab king of Samaria. And after this Ahab said to Naboth, "Give me your vineyard, that I may have it for a vegetable garden, because it is near my house ..." But Naboth said to Ahab, "The Lord forbid that I should give you the inheritance of my fathers" ...' 1 Kings 21: 1-3

It was Ahab's wife Jezebel who then took matters into her own hands. Naboth was quoting the law which protected the people from just such arbitrary acts of despotism and land-grabbing. But Jezebel cared nothing for the law; it took Elijah's words to reduce Ahab to repentance — and God's judgement to put an end to Jezebel's evil influence.

Ahab's Palace

'So the king died, and was brought to Samaria; and they buried the king in Samaria. And they washed the chariot by the pool of Samaria, and the dogs licked up his blood, and the harlots washed themselves in it, according to the word of the Lord which he had spoken. Now the rest of the acts of Ahab, and all that he did, and the ivory house which he built, and all the cities that he built, are they not written in the Book of the Chronicles of the Kings of Israel?'
1 Kings 22: 37-39

The magnificent hill-top city of Samaria was built by Omri and made his capital. Ahab erected a temple to Baal there, and then built a luxurious palace. More than 200 pieces of ivory were discovered in a store-room, during the excavation of the site. This picture shows the remains of the palace itself, high up on the hill among ruins from the time of the Roman occupation, centuries later. A 10-yard-long pool, probably the one in which Ahab's blood-stained chariot was washed down, has also been uncovered. The prophet Amos, about a hundred years later, tells of people who 'feel secure on the mountain of Samaria . . . who lie upon beds of ivory', and goes on to depict their downfall.

The chariot cities

'Ben-hadad the king of Syria gathered all his army together; thirty-two kings were with him, and horses and chariots; and he went up and besieged Samaria, and fought against it. And he sent messengers into the city to Ahab king of Israel, and said to him, "Thus says Ben-hadad: 'Your silver and your gold are mine; your fairest wives and children also are mine.'"...'*
1 Kings 20: 1-3

The threat of Ben-hadad, for all his bravado, was fought off, both in the hills and later on the plain. Chariots featured, too, in Ahab's battle with Shalmaneser III at Qarqar: according to Shalmaneser Ahab had a force of 2,000 chariots. The picture shows the remains of the stables for his horses at Megiddo. The water-troughs and hitching-posts, also from Megiddo, are shown erected in the picture below, taken at the Rockefeller Museum, Jerusalem. Solomon had established Megiddo, Hazor and Gezer as chariot-cities: 'he had fourteen hundred chariots and twelve thousand horsemen, whom he stationed in the chariot cities and with the king in Jerusalem' (1 Kings 10: 26).

The siege of Samaria

'Then the king of Assyria invaded all the land and came to Samaria, and for three years he besieged it. In the ninth year of Hoshea the king of Assyria captured Samaria, and he carried the Israelites away to Assyria ... And this was so, because the people of Israel had sinned against the Lord their God, who had brought them up out of the land of Egypt from under the hand of Pharaoh king of Egypt, and had feared other gods and walked in the customs of the nations whom the Lord drove out before the people of Israel, and in the customs which the kings of Israel had introduced. And the people of Israel did secretly against the Lord their God things that were not right ...' 2 Kings 17: 5-9

The prophets had warned the people of the coming invasion, warned them to turn from their sin and from the judgement to come. The threat from Assyria, for so long just over the horizon, became an ugly reality. The crumbling walls on the heights of Samaria look down over a scene which, in 722 BC, saw the culmination of three years of siege. The city fell. The people were deported. The area was repopulated by Assyria with other conquered peoples. These inter-married with the few Israelites who were left, forming the Samaritan people so despised and hated in the time of Jesus, and surviving today as a few hundred people with their own traditions and worship.

Lachish

'In the fourteenth year of King Hezekiah Sennacherib king of Assyria came up against all the fortified cities of Judah and took them. And Hezekiah king of Judah sent to the king of Assyria at Lachish, saying, "I have done wrong; withdraw from me; whatever you impose on me I will bear." And the king of Assyria required of Hezekiah king of Judah three hundred talents of silver and thirty talents of gold. And Hezekiah gave him all the silver that was found in the house of the Lord, and in the treasuries of the king's house.'
2 Kings 18: 13-15

Eight years after the fall of Samaria and the exile of the northern kingdom of Israel, the Assyrians attack Judah to the south. Lachish, a fortified city in the foot-hills of Judah in the approaches to Jerusalem, had first to be immobilized before the capital itself. The 'tell', or mound of Lachish, can be seen in the distance in the picture. The smaller picture shows the remains on top of the mound. Joshua had taken Lachish in an attack lasting two days: signs of burning from that time can still be seen. The fortifications were strengthened under Rehoboam. The siege by the Assyrian general Sennacherib was vividly portrayed in reliefs on the walls of his palace at Nineveh (now in the British Museum). The heavy destruction was shown in the remains discovered by archaeologists — and by a mass grave holding 1,500 bodies. With Lachish wiped out and the line of support from Egypt thus cut off, Sennacherib marched on Jerusalem.

The defence of Jerusalem

'Then Isaiah said to Hezekiah, "Hear the word of the Lord; Behold, the days are coming, when all that is in your house, and that which your fathers have stored up till this day, shall be carried to Babylon; nothing shall be left, says the Lord ..." The rest of the deeds of Hezekiah, and all his might, and how he made the pool and the conduit and brought water into the city, are they not written in the Book of the Chronicles of the Kings of Judah? And Hezekiah slept with his fathers; and Manasseh his son reigned in his stead ...'
2 Kings 20: 16-17, 20-21

As king of Judah, Hezekiah had initiated thorough and widespread reforms. He reopened the Temple and established its services, attacked pagan practices, undertook extensive rebuilding and the fortification of Jerusalem against the threat of invasion. One of his measures was to ensure that there was access inside the city walls to water from one of Jerusalem's principal water-supplies, the Gihon spring, pictured here. To do so he dug a tunnel 1,750 feet through solid rock from the spring to bring the water to a pool (the Pool of Siloam) inside the walls. The tunnel was discovered in 1880, including an inscription (now in the Istanbul Archaeological Museum) graphically recording the event. Hezekiah won a reprieve for Jerusalem: the city was not destroyed until the attack of Nebuchadnezzar of Babylon in 587 BC.

Return to Jerusalem

'So I came to Jerusalem and was there three days. Then I arose in the night, I and a few men with me; and I told no one what my God had put into my heart to do for Jerusalem . . . Then I said to them, "You see the trouble we are in, how Jerusalem lies in ruins with its gates burned. Come, let us build the wall of Jerusalem, that we may no longer suffer disgrace." And I told them of the hand of my God which had been upon me for good, and also of the words which the king had spoken to me. And they said, "Let us rise up and build."'
Nehemiah 2: 11, 12, 17, 18

Nehemiah in exile was cupbearer to the king of Persia. In this influential position he was able to take action following reports he had heard of the state of Jerusalem. A man of prayer, he was also a man of great organizational ability. Despite opposition, under his leadership the people rebuilt the walls of Jerusalem in under two months. Nehemiah was appointed governor in 445 BC, went back to Persia for a time, and returned later to reform abuses that had arisen in his absence. With Ezra, he re-established worship and obedience to the law of God.

Most of the present walls of Jerusalem date from medieval times. Some of the massive masonry from Herod's Temple survives. This was started in 19 BC and finished only a few years before its destruction by the Romans in AD 70. This picture shows the 'Golden Gate', in the position of the one east-facing gate of Herod's Temple.

LEBANON

Tyre ▲

▲ Hazor

GALILEE

River Jordan

SAMARIA

Mountains of Samaria

Gibeon ▲

▲ **Jerusalem**

Judean Mountains

▲ Massada

Negev Desert

▲ Avdat

PART FOUR

Poets and Prophets

Job

*'There was a man in the land of Uz,
whose name was Job; and that man
was blameless and upright, one who
feared God, and turned away from
evil. There were born to him seven sons
and three daughters. He had seven
thousand sheep, three thousand camels,
five hundred yoke of oxen, and five
hundred she-asses, and very many
servants; so that this man was the
greatest of all the people of the east.
His sons used to go and hold a feast
in the house of each on his day; and they
would send and invite their three sisters
to eat and drink with them. And when the
days of the feast had run their course,
Job would send and sanctify them, and
he would rise early in the morning and
offer burnt offerings according to the
number of them all; for Job said, "It may
be that my sons have sinned, and cursed
God in their hearts." Thus Job did
continually.'* Job 1: 1-5

We do not know who wrote the book of
Job, or when and where it was written.
It is tempting to think it was the product
of fireside storytelling, told and retold
since the patriarchal times in which it
was set. It may, however, have arisen
out of the much more sophisticated
environment that also produced
Proverbs and Ecclesiastes, as an
intellectual protest against the religious
dogmatism and blinkered theology which
reduced God to a set of rules. It may
have seemed obvious that when Job lost
his wealth and his ten children and was
stricken with illness, it was God judging
him for his sins. This is what his friends
said. But that was not the answer . . .

The Lord is my Shepherd

'The Lord is my shepherd,
I shall not want;
he makes me lie down in green pastures.
He leads me beside still waters;
he restores my soul.
He leads me in paths of righteousness
for his name's sake.
Even though I walk through the valley
of the shadow of death,
I fear no evil;
for thou art with me;
thy rod and thy staff,
they comfort me . . .' Psalm 23

The Psalms were both the hymn-book and anthology of poetry of Israel. They include hymns for religious occasions, such as the 'songs of ascents', sung by the worshippers in procession behind the ark at a festival. Others had titles suggesting they were for thanksgiving or lament or teaching. Many are very personal, the expression of trust, or despair, or joy, or wonder. A picture of sheep grazing in lush meadows beside still waters is not an easy one to find in the lands of the Middle East. It was an ideal, a beautiful picture of peace and security. For the one whose shepherd is God himself it can be realized even in conditions which are less than ideal — even among enemies and facing the threat of danger and death.

Gazelles on the mountains

*'As a hart longs
for flowing streams,
so longs my soul
for thee, O God.
My soul thirsts for God,
for the living God.
When shall I come and behold
the face of God?
My tears have been my food
day and night,
while man say to me continually,
"Where is your God?" '* Psalm 42: 1-3

The Psalms are rich with imagery from
the countryside and desert. These
gazelles are in the gorge of Avdat, in
the Negev desert in the south of Israel.
Hart, or deer, are no longer to be found
in Israel—the last disappeared early
this century. In the desert it is only too
easy to appreciate the aching longing
for water expressed in the psalm, which
the poet uses to picture his longing for
renewed fellowship with God.

Mount Zion

*'Great is the Lord and greatly to be praised
in the city of our God! . . .
Walk about Zion, go round about her,
number her towers,
consider well her ramparts,
go through her citadels;
that you may tell the next generation
that this is God,
our God for ever and ever.'* Psalm 48: 1, 12-14

Mount Zion was one of the hills of
Jerusalem. Traditionally the name has
been referred to the one pictured here;
but David's City itself was further to the
east, and it is clear that Zion included the
religious centre of Israel, the Temple.
So it can be generally equated with
Jerusalem, the aspiration of every
pilgrim, the stronghold of Israel, the
symbol of the nation under God.

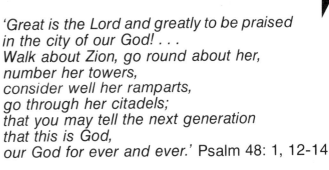

Massada, the fortress

'He who dwells in the shelter of the Most High,
who abides in the shadow of the Almighty,
will say to the Lord, "My refuge and my fortress;
my God, in whom I trust." . . .
His faithfulness is a shield and buckler.
You will not fear the terror of the night,
nor the arrow that flies by day,
nor the pestilence that stalks in darkness,
nor the destruction that wastes at noonday.'
Psalm 91: 1-6

Just over two miles from the Dead Sea, in the rocky Wilderness of Judea, rises the great rock slab of Massada, or Metsuda, a fortress or stronghold. Here the Jews made their last heroic stand against the Romans in AD 73. After three years of siege, the defenders put themselves to death rather than fall into enemy hands. Several times in the Psalms David calls the Lord his fortress. It may have been to this place that he came when fleeing from Saul: 'David and his men went up to the stronghold.' In any case it was a powerful image of the fact that God would not only defend him but himself be his refuge and fortress. At Massada today can be seen storehouses, reservoirs and fortifications from the time of the Jewish Revolt; also remains of a palace built by Herod, and ruins of a Roman fort.

Wisdom in the streets

'Wisdom cries aloud in the street;
in the markets she raises her voice;
on the top of the walls she cries out;
at the entrance of the city gates she
speaks:
"How long, O simple ones, will you love
being simple?
How long will scoffers delight in their
scoffing
and fools hate knowledge?
Give heed to my reproof . . ." '
Proverbs 1: 20-23

The Old Testament 'wisdom literature'
includes Proverbs, Job and
Ecclesiastes. Job was written in the form
of a great poetic drama. Proverbs is at
the other literary extreme, consisting of
a collection of short pithy thoughts. But
the basic concern is the same: to seek
out what is true in life. In Proverbs this
is expressed in the form of 'wise sayings'
expressing what is 'true in general',
what is normally the case in ordinary,
daily life. They are not so much promises
from God as descriptions of life under
God. Idleness, falsehood, dishonesty,
crooked dealing, adultery are not the
way to wisdom and life. Trusting in God,
living a life that is consistent with the way
he has been created, this is how man
has been designed to live and so the way
to true success and happiness.

Overgrown vineyard

'I passed by the field of a sluggard,
by the vineyard of a man without sense;
and lo, it was all overgrown with thorns;
the ground was covered with nettles,
and its stone wall was broken down.
Then I saw and considered it;
I looked and received instruction.
A little sleep, a little slumber,
a little folding of the hands to rest,
and poverty will come upon you like a
robber,
and want like an armed man.'
Proverbs 24: 30-34

In graphic, humorous detail the point is made. Laziness inevitably leads to ruin. Again, this is what is usually the case; it is a simple observation of life. The nations around Israel at this time also had their 'wisdom books', such as the Egyptian *Wisdom of Amenemope*. Some have concluded that the Bible's wisdom is therefore no more than imitation. But the whole point of wisdom literature was to distil what is universally true. If this has been well expressed by secular man, then its truth can be underlined. But 'wisdom' which does not relate human life to the one who created and sustains it is not truly wise; for the 'fear of the Lord is the beginning of wisdom'.

Life under the sun

'Vanity of vanities, says the Preacher,
vanity of vanities! All is vanity.
What does man gain by all the toil
at which he toils under the sun?
A generation goes, and a generation
comes,
but the earth remains for ever.
The sun rises and the sun goes down,
and hastens to the place where it rises ...
All things are full of weariness ...
and there is nothing new under the sun.'
Ecclesiastes 1: 2-9

Life without God is vain, empty, fruitless. The seasons come and go, nothing changes, nothing is new. In love or war, toil or leisure, life goes on, life 'under the sun' is apparently pointless, meaningless. If all this has a twentieth-century ring to it, it is not by accident. For 'the Preacher' was doing what many twentieth-century writers are also doing: expressing the cynicism and meaninglessness of man and the daily round. But Ecclesiastes also introduces a wider perspective, that of life under God — though he scarcely begins to give the answers. As the Bible makes plain, these await the coming of the One who can make all things new.

Song of songs

'I am very dark, but comely,
O daughters of Jerusalem,
like the tents of Kedar,
like the curtains of Solomon.
Do not gaze at me because I am swarthy,
because the sun has scorched me.
My mother's sons were angry with me,
they made me keeper of the vineyards;
but, my own vineyard I have not kept!
Tell me, you whom my soul loves,
where you pasture your flock,
where you make it lie down at noon;
for why should I be like one who wanders
beside the flocks of your companions?'
Song of Solomon 1: 5-7

The Bible's collection of poetry and wisdom would be incomplete without the pure lyric feeling and joy in love expressed in the Song of Solomon. It is difficult to unravel the 'story' expressed in the dialogue between bridegroom and bride. Some see it as the tale of a beautiful country girl taken to the King's court, who is torn between the royal suitor and her rustic lover. But it may be that it is simply a collection of love-songs grouped together with little connection. What is clear is that the Bible contains in this book a celebration of the purity, beauty and wonder of human love. It was Greek philosophy that introduced the idea that physical love belongs to the lower nature, and that things of the soul have no connection with things of the body. The Bible sees no such division. The God who created man to love him also created man and woman and their love for one another.

Scarlet dye

'Come now, let us reason together,
says the Lord:
though your sins are like scarlet,
they shall be as white as snow;
though they are red like crimson,
they shall become like wool.' Isaiah 1: 18

After Solomon's death, the unity and
wealth of the kingdom was disrupted by
civil war and the division of the kingdom
into north and south, Judah and Israel.
By Isaiah's time, Judah under King Uzziah
(who reigned about 790-740 BC) was
again prosperous. The danger was not
civil war or even invasion but the sins
of luxury and self-indulgence. Whatever
the danger and whatever the sin, Isaiah
remained faithful to his prophetic
message, recalling men from evil and
promising God's forgiveness in response
to repentance and faith.

Tyre and Sidon

'Wail, O ships of Tarshish,
for Tyre is laid waste, without house or
haven! . . .
Be ashamed, O Sidon . . .' Isaiah 23: 1, 4

The Phoenicians of Tyre and Sidon were
indeed the merchants and seafarers of
the nations. Isaiah's prophecy about
Sidon (pictured here) came about when
the Assyrians under Sennacherib marched
on the city and defeated it. Much of
Isaiah's book is concerned with the
nations around, both inveighing against
their immorality and warning of the
dangers of invasion or alliance. Because
of their strategic importance in com-
merce and communications, Sidon and
Tyre (pictured on page 84) continued
to be dominated by foreign powers, down
to Roman times. It was here that
Jesus healed the daughter of the Syro-
Phoenician woman, and many listened
to his teaching there.

131

Water in the desert

'When the poor and needy seek water,
and there is none,
and their tongue is parched with thirst,
I the Lord will answer them,
I the God of Israel will not forsake them.
I will open rivers on the bare heights,
and fountains in the midst of the valleys;
I will make the wilderness a pool of water,
and the dry land springs of water . . .
that men may see and know,
may consider and understand together,
that the hand of the Lord has done this,
the Holy One of Israel has created it.'
Isaiah 41: 17, 18, 20

From political intrigue and the threat of invasion, from the horrors of war and exile, Isaiah called the people to lift up their eyes to a future in which God would wipe away their tears, the land would be restored to them and God would dwell in harmony with his people. In a country with such a large proportion of barren desert, it was natural for the symbol of this messianic rule to become 'the desert that blossomed'.

Gehenna

'For the sons of Judah have done evil in my sight, says the Lord; they have set their abominations in the house which is called by my name, to defile it. And they have built the high place of Topheth, which is in the valley of the son of Hinnom, to burn their sons and their daughters in the fire; which I did not command, nor did it come into my mind. Therefore, behold, the days are coming, says the Lord, when it will no more be called Topheth, or the valley of the son of Hinnom, but the valley of Slaughter: . . . And I will make to cease from the cities of Judah and from the streets of Jerusalem the voice of mirth and the voice of gladness, the voice of the bridegroom and the voice of the bride; for the land shall become a waste.'
Jeremiah 7: 30-32, 34

Jeremiah is generally associated with gloom and disaster: but as a sensitive and gentle man this was the last sort of message that he wanted to bring. It is a measure of his utter faithfulness that he stuck to his calling regardless of personal misfortune. The Valley of Hinnom, pictured here, curves round the south-western side of the city of Jerusalem. In Jeremiah's time it was associated with the evils of child-sacrifice. It was also to become the city rubbish-dump, where the refuse was continually burning. The name Hinnom, or Gehenna, became a symbol of hell itself.

The potter

'The word that came to Jeremiah from the Lord: "Arise, and go down to the potter's house, and there I will let you hear my words." So I went down to the potter's house, and there he was working at his wheel. And the vessel he was making of clay was spoiled in the potter's hand, and he reworked it into another vessel, as it seemed good to the potter to do.
Then the word of the Lord came to me: "O house of Israel, can I not do with you as this potter has done?"'
Jeremiah 18: 1-6

As the lump of clay is turned on the wheel, it is formed by the potter's hand into a jar or bowl. This was a vivid picture of the way God 'moulds' his people, and one that recurs in the Bible. Equally, as here, the pot that did not shape up as intended could be scrapped and started again. 'Behold, like the clay in the potter's hand, so are you in my hand, O house of Israel.'

A basket of figs

'After Nebuchadrezzar king of Babylon had taken into exile from Jerusalem Jeconiah the son of Jehoiakim, king of Judah, together with the princes of Judah, the craftsmen, and the smiths, and had brought them to Babylon, the Lord showed me this vision: Behold, two baskets of figs placed before the temple of the Lord. One basket had very good figs, like first-ripe figs, but the other basket had very bad figs, so bad that they could not be eaten. And the Lord said to me, "What do you see, Jeremiah?" I said, "Figs, the good figs very good, and the bad figs very bad, so bad that they cannot be eaten."'
Jeremiah 24: 1-3

Many of the prophecies were delivered in striking pictorial terms. (Ezekiel in exile even built models under the fascinated gaze of his watchers.) Nebuchadrezzar had put on the throne of Judah a puppet-king, Zedekiah—the Old Testament account of this is supported by the Babylonian Chronicle. The new king banished the previous leaders of the nation and surrounded himself with poor substitutes—Jeremiah's 'good and bad figs'. The prophet risked his neck for his outspokenness: God would renew his covenant with his faithful, exiled people, but Zedekiah and his princes would be utterly destroyed.

The pool at Gibeon

'In the seventh month, Ishmael . . . came with ten men to Gedaliah the son of Ahikam, at Mizpah. As they ate bread together there at Mizpah, Ishmael the son of Nethaniah and the ten men with him rose up and struck down Gedaliah the son of Ahikam, son of Shaphan, with the sword, and killed him, whom the king of Babylon had appointed governor in the land . . . But when Johanan the son of Kareah and all the leaders of the forces with him heard of all the evil which Ishmael the son of Nethaniah had done, they took all their men and went to fight against Ishmael the son of Nethaniah. They came upon him at the great pool which is in Gibeon.'
Jeremiah 41: 1, 2, 11, 12

Excavations at a site about 6 miles north of Jerusalem revealed a large pit with stairs leading down to a tunnel. The tunnel leads to a well outside the walls of the city. In the pit were jars inscribed with the name of the city: Gibeon. The events of the 'great pool of Gibeon' were part of the tangled aftermath of the Babylonian invasion, the murder of the governor Gedaliah being followed by the counter-attack and eventual flight to Egypt — Jeremiah being unwillingly taken along with the rest.

The Wailing Wall

'How lonely sits the city
that was full of people!
How like a widow has she become,
she that was great among the nations!
She that was a princess among the cities
has become a vassal . . .
But thou, O Lord, dost reign for ever;
thy throne endures to all generations.
Why dost thou forget us for ever,
why dost thou so long forsake us?
Restore us to thyself, O Lord, that we may
be restored!
Renew our days as of old!
Or hast thou utterly rejected us?
Art thou exceedingly angry with us?'
Lamentations 1: 1; 5: 19-22

The beginning and end of Lamentations
sum up the aspirations of a people denied
their spiritual home: 'How long, O Lord . . .'
The Wailing Wall, or Western Wall of the
former Temple in Jerusalem, has been
the focus of the sorrow and hope of the
dispersed people of Israel down to the
present day. Since Israel's repossession
of the wall it has become a shrine and
symbol of national renewal.

The cedar tree

'Thus says the Lord God: "I myself will take a sprig from the lofty top of the cedar, and will set it out; I will break off from the topmost of its young twigs a tender one, and I myself will plant it upon a high and lofty mountain: on the mountain height of Israel will I plant it, that it may bring forth boughs and bear fruit, and become a noble cedar; and under it will dwell all kinds of beasts; in the shade of its branches birds of every sort will nest. And all the trees of the field shall know that I the Lord bring low the high tree, and make high the low tree, dry up the green tree, and make the dry tree flourish. I the Lord have spoken, and I will do it." '
Ezekiel 17: 22-24

Ezekiel, deported to Babylon, was called to be a prophet when he was thirty — the age at which, under normal circumstances, he would have been received into the priesthood. With emotional intensity and vivid symbolism he expressed the concern and longing of an exile for his land and the nation's spiritual renewal. On the day that Jerusalem fell, Ezekiel's wife died, summing up the complete personal identification of the prophet with the subject of his message. His oracle about the cedar of Lebanon and the eagle which took a branch from its top is typical of his soaring prophetic imagination. Today the magnificent cedars of Lebanon, once the source of timber for Solomon's Temple, are reduced to a few isolated groves of trees high in the mountains.

The watchman

*'So you, son of man, I have made a
watchman for the house of Israel; when-
ever you hear a word from my mouth,
you shall give them warning from me.
If I say to the wicked, O wicked man, you
shall surely die, and you do not speak to
warn the wicked to turn from his way,
that wicked man shall die in his iniquity,
but his blood I will require at your hand.
But if you warn the wicked to turn from
his way, and he does not turn from his
way; he shall die in his iniquity, but
you will have saved your life.'*
Ezekiel 33: 7-9

Small towers from which watchmen can
keep guard over valuable crops and olive-
groves are a familiar sight among the
hills of Judah and Samaria. With char-
acteristic concern, Ezekiel sees his role
as a matter of life and death. If as
watchman he fails to warn the people of
their impending fate, their blood would
be on his head. Such earnestness and
utter dedication was typical of the
'prophets of the Lord'; theirs was a key
role, carrying heavy responsibility both
to God and to his people.

Return, O Israel

*'Return, O Israel, to the Lord your God,
for you have stumbled because of your
iniquity . . .
I will heal their faithlessness;
I will love them freely,
for my anger has turned from them.
I will be as the dew to Israel;
he shall blossom as the lily,
he shall strike root as the poplar;
his shoots shall spread out;
his beauty shall be like the olive,
and his fragrance like Lebanon.
They shall return and dwell beneath my
shadow,
they shall flourish as a garden;
they shall blossom as the vine,
their fragrance shall be like the wine of
Lebanon.'* Hosea 14: 1, 4-7

Hosea was another prophet deeply iden-
tified with his message. As a northerner,
he loved the land and its gentle land--
scapes, like this peaceful scene in Galilee.
He also loved his wife, and it was her
unfaithfulness which showed him how
agonizing it was to God that his people
should be unfaithful and rebellious. He
shows God's love for his people, his longing to forgive them, his longing to restore
them to the peace and content expressed
in the picture of lily and poplar, olive
and vine.

The ploughman

' "Behold, the days are coming," says the
Lord,
"when the ploughman shall overtake the reaper
and the treader of grapes him who
sows the seed;
the mountains shall drip sweet wine,
and all the hills shall flow with it.
I will restore the fortunes of my people Israel,
and they shall rebuild the ruined cities
and inhabit them;
they shall plant vineyards and drink their wine,
and they shall make gardens and eat their fruit.
I will plant them upon their land,
and they shall never again be plucked up
out of the land which I have given them,"
says the Lord your God.' Amos 9: 13-15

Amos was a countryman sickened by
the corruption, immorality and social
inequality of Samaria, capital city of
Israel. In calling the people to
repentance and righteousness he was
unpopular and ignored. Only in these last
verses of his prophecy does he allow
a hope for the future to shine through.
In rural areas of the Middle East today
a wooden plough is still used, drawn
by a horse or by oxen.

A pagan shrine

'And in that day, says the Lord, . . .
I will cut off sorceries from your hand,
and you shall have no more soothsayers;
and I will cut off your images
and your pillars from among you,
and you shall bow down no more
to the work of your hands; . . .
With what shall I come before the Lord,
and bow myself before God on high? . . .
He has showed you, O man, what is good;
and what does the Lord require of you
but to do justice, and to love kindness,
and to walk humbly with your God?'
Micah 5:10, 12, 13; 6: 6, 8

The prophets combined demands for social justice with denunciation of the evils of pagan religion. For immorality fed on paganism, wanton disregard for human values on a religion which had no moral concern. This altar at Byblos, Lebanon was dedicated to pagan practices going back to Canaanite times.

The storehouse

'Will man rob God? Yet you are robbing me. But you say, "How are we robbing thee?" In your tithes and offerings. You are cursed with a curse, for you are robbing me; the whole nation of you. Bring the full tithes into the storehouse, that there may be food in my house; and thereby put me to the test, says the Lord of hosts, if I will not open the windows of heaven for you and pour down for you an overflowing blessing. I will rebuke the devourer for you, so that it will not destroy the fruits of your soil; and your vine in the field shall not fail to bear, says the Lord of hosts. Then all nations will call you blessed, for you will be a land of delight, says the Lord of hosts.' Malachi 3: 8-12

The pillars of a building at Hazor, in northern Galilee, are thought to have belonged to a storehouse. A rural economy depended to a large extent on storage of oil and grain, and the storehouse to Malachi was a test of the people's devotion to God. Then, as now, it was a question of whether the people would show where their heart was by putting their money there also. Throughout Old Testament times, the choice was simple, but difficult. Will man love God with all his heart and soul and all he is, following the ways of his law and his creation? Or will he go his own way, with all the disastrous results recorded in Old Testament history? Today the choice is as acutely necessary as ever.